How to Raise and Train a
PET HAMSTER

by Mervin F. Roberts

Photographs by the author

The author gratefully acknowledges the help of Dr. H. D. Burdick, Dr. Joseph G. Fortner, Miss Alice Gale, Mr. William Lees, Mr. Joseph Stocker, Mr. Van Densen and Dr. Van Gelder.

ISBN 0-87666-205-X

Manufactured in the United States of America
Library of Congress Catalog Card No.: 58-12554

Distributed in the U.S. by T.F.H. Publications, Inc., 211 West Sylvania Avenue, P.O. Box 427, Neptune, N.J. 07753; in England by T.F.H. (Gt. Britain) Ltd., 13 Nutley Lane, Reigate, Surrey; in Canada to the book store and library trade by Beaverbooks, 953 Dillingham Road, Pickering, Ontario L1W 1Z7; in Canada to the pet trade by Rolf C. Hagen Ltd., 3225 Sartelon Street, Montreal 382, Quebec; in Southeast Asia by Y.W. Ong, 9 Lorong 36 Geylang, Singapore 14; in Australia and the South Pacific by Pet Imports Pty. Ltd., P.O. Box 149, Brookvale 2100, N.S.W., Australia; in South Africa by Valiant Publishers (Pty.) Ltd., P.O. Box 78236, Sandton City, 2146, South Africa; Published by T.F.H. Publications, Inc., Ltd., The British Crown Colony of Hong Kong.

CONTENTS

This male golden hamster is stuffing his pouches with sunflower seeds that his owner holds loosely in her hand.

Note the erect ears and full body on this young adult female.

1. WHAT IS A HAMSTER?

Many books about pets start with an apology of some sort. Your parakeet (they say) is really a budgerigar. A guinea pig is not a pig from Guinea but a cavy. A pet chameleon is actually an anolis. An alligator is probably a caiman. And don't be surprised, you're told, if some rabbits are really hares.

But here is a book about a hamster, which is exactly and precisely a hamster. It has a perfectly legitimate Latin name—*Mesocricetus auratus auratus*—but even the scientists just call it a hamster.

The pet animal illustrated and described in these pages is one of six subspecies of the golden hamster. Some people call one color variety of pet hamsters "Syrian hamsters," but this can be confusing because, although the golden hamsters do come from Syria, there are still other hamsters that come from there too.

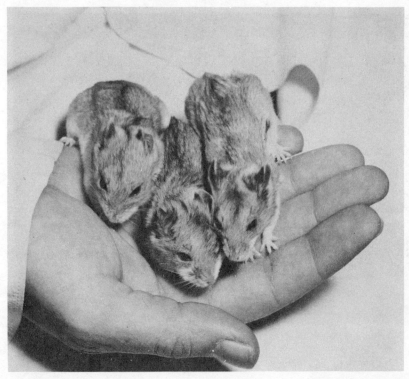

Photo by Jimmy Fund.

These charming little animals are Chinese hamsters, Cricetulus griseus. Today they are laboratory rarities, but the author predicts that they will soon become popular pets.

Golden hamsters have soft golden-red fur over their backs and sides. Darker marks, or flashes, appear on foreheads and cheeks. Bellies are bluish-gray to white, and through selective breeding they are becoming whiter. Markings are uniform on all animals, but variations in the fur color occur in various strains.

The hamster's skin is very loose on its body (it can be pulled over an inch from almost every part of the body). Eyes are bright and bold and curious, but eyesight is not keen. The feet are good at grasping. The tail is merely a stump, about one-quarter of an inch long. The remainder of a full-grown hamster extends for about five or six inches.

An unusual feature of hamsters, setting them apart from most other animals, is the cheek pouch, which is used for gathering food and litter for nests, or for preparing the nest litter. The pouches extend from the cheeks to the shoulders and can hold food approximately equal to one-half of the animal's volume. The inside is a soft tissue which slightly moistens the material being stored. The pouches are not evident except when they are full and the animal is viewed from above.

The story of the golden hamster as a *pet* began in 1930 when the late Professor I. Aharoni of the Department of Zoology of Hebrew University, Jerusalem, acquired an adult female and her litter of 12 babies near Aleppo, Syria. A few months afterward, he gave one male and two females of the wild litter to the university and there Ben-Menahem first bred them. This trio is believed to be the source of every living golden hamster in captivity today. Some of the young were sent to England in 1931, and from there a few were shipped to the United States Public Health Service Research Station at Carville, Louisiana, where they were used for medical research.

It was the research scientists who first noticed that hamsters made fine pets, and it was probably from the stock at Carville that hamsters became available to the public. By now there are certainly more golden hamsters in captivity than there are in all the hamster burrows in Syria.

This fellow's cheek pouches are about two-thirds full, and he's still going strong.

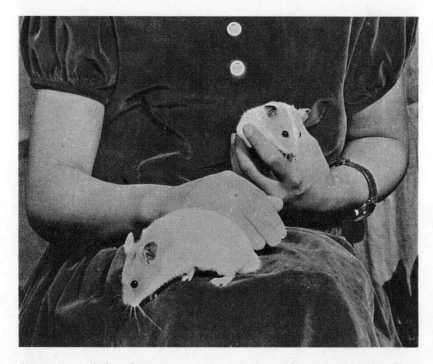

Among the varieties of hamsters are these dark-eyed fawn-colored pandas. They have hardly any white or dark hair. They can be mated with other color varieties since they are all of the same species.

Why Have a Hamster as a Pet?

In a relatively short time, hamsters have become very popular as pets. And for good reason. Today there are millions of hamsters giving affection and amusement to their owners. The fact that they are easy to care for, gentle, attractive, and very entertaining makes them especially suitable as pets in small quarters.

Hamsters are small animals, larger than mice but smaller than rats. One or two can easily be kept in a bird cage.

Hamsters are amusing animals. They sit up, stand on their hind legs, sit like bears and climb and grasp practically anything they can get their "hands" on. They can grasp with their hind feet as well, and enjoy doing acrobatic tricks.

Hamsters are gentle, clean, odorless, and practically mute.

While most pets need daily care, hamsters can be left alone over a weekend, if necessary, because they hoard food and don't drink much.

The hamsters' hoarding habit, incidentally, is what makes them especially interesting to watch. (The name comes from the German *hamstern,* meaning "to hoard.") You will be fascinated as you watch a hamster stuff food into his enormous cheek pouches, and then take it out and hide it "for a rainy day."

Hamsters are handsome little animals, and they come in several colors.

They are inexpensive—you can probably buy a hamster for a dollar or two.

They are easy to breed, and, with a minimum of care, resistant to disease.

Their life span is about 1000 days—almost three years.

They enjoy being hand fed, played with and fondled. Their fur is soft and pleasant to touch. If one escapes, he will probably be happy to return to his cage.

It is no wonder hamsters have become so popular so quickly!

"I can't eat another bite!" The carrot-eating hamster's pouches are almost stuffed full. He should now unload his cargo so it doesn't stick or spoil.

2. HOW TO CHOOSE A HAMSTER

If you've never seen a hamster, visit your nearest pet shop and ask to see some. A few minutes of observation will probably convince you that it would be fun to own one. The next step is to choose the one for you.

The quickest way to a hamster's heart is through his stomach. When you buy your hamster, choose one that is friendly and can be handled easily.

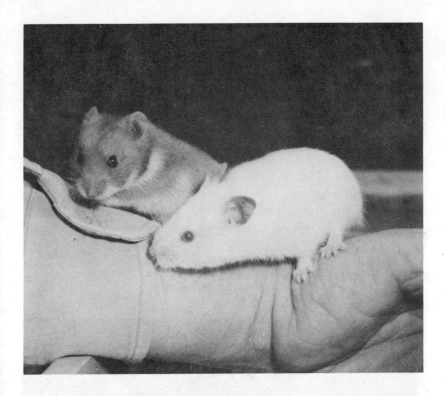

The albino hamster resembles his golden hamster cousin except for color. Their habits are the same and they can be mated with each other.

Age

It is best to get your hamster just a few weeks after it has been weaned away from its mother—at about 5 weeks of age. Luckily, however, the golden hamster is so gentle and so easily tamed that even a year-old animal can be trained without too much difficulty. But there's another good reason for choosing a baby, if you're being really practical. Since hamsters live only about a thousand days, and cost about a dollar or two, you can figure that a year-old hamster has already lived out between 30 and 60 cents of your investment. On the other hand, a hamster younger than 30 days is too young to move, too young to play with, too young to have good control of its emotions or its locomotion. Baby hamsters have poor vision and those under 30 days will have a great deal of trouble seeing things—the edge of a table, for instance. While older hamsters will come to the edge of a table and stop,

11

the baby will often go right over the edge and topple to the floor. This is dangerous because, unlike mice, hamsters don't seem to be able to flick about in the air and fall lightly on their feet.

Sex

Your hamster can be of either sex, since both males and females make good pets. A pair could make thousands of good pets. A word of warning, though: don't buy a pair unless you know in advance what you are going to do with the babies. Pet shops can probably obtain exactly what the market calls for, when there is a demand, more readily from commercial breeders than from individuals such as you. Don't plan to make your pet pay for itself. Few pets do.

This adult male has a dimorphic pigment spot on his hip. It is normal — somewhat like a human's "beauty mark."

You can teach your hamster to sit up and beg for sunflower seeds. A balanced diet, with some treats added, will keep him well fed but not fat.

Your hamster's eyes should be large, bright and prominent.

Appearance

The size of your pet when you buy it is primarily dependent on its age. However, it should weigh 45 grams (about an ounce and a half) or more. A hamster smaller than that will have the same trouble as a very young one. The shape and general appearance of the hamster you choose is very important. Lumps, bumps, discoloration, loose hair, wet bottom or tail, stuffed or running nose, running eyes, blood anywhere and bad disposition are all symptoms which should stop you from making a purchase. Don't buy anything but a perfectly healthy pet! Then you can look forward to keeping it free from disease for the next thousand days or so. The signs of good health are soft, silken fur, plump body, a general feeling of solidity to the body, prominent bright eyes, and an alert inquisitiveness.

Some hamsters, especially older males, have one or two black dots over their hips under the skin. Each is about as large as the

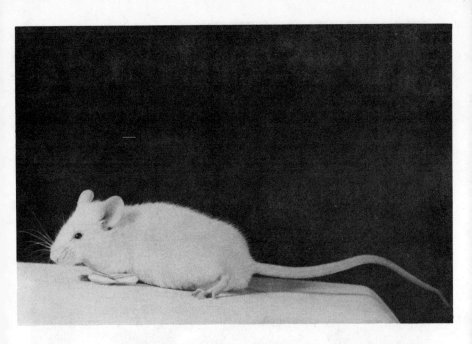

(Above) Here, for comparison, is a mouse. Its face is much narrower than the hamster's; its tail much longer. (Below) Hamsters are such clean animals that even a snow-white albino is always spotless.

The albino is completely white, with pink eyes.

The male golden hamster is the larger animal on the left. Notice that the female's ears are erect. If she lays them back—watch out!

This pied hamster is spotted beige, with brown eyes.

Pied hamsters are the result of genetic mutation. No two are marked exactly alike.

This, too, is a pied hamster. He has no black fur at all, and his spots are rather evenly distributed.

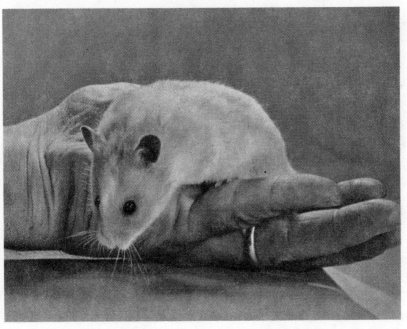

hamster's eye and about two or three times the thickness of the skin. These are quite normal. They are called dimorphic pigment spots and are much like "beauty marks" in humans. Some perfectly healthy hamsters will lick these spots in warm weather. Large lumps, boils, abscesses and pimples are another matter, of course.

Another bulge to watch for, on females, is the bulge of pregnancy. If a female hamster was in a cage of mixed sexes, the chances are good that she will have babies within 16 days.

A tiny nick or hole on a hamster's ear may be a breeder's mark, or it may be the result of a bite from the hamster's cagemate. It is not a disease, and unless you plan to exhibit your pet in a competitive show you can ignore it.

The hamster you choose should have a gentle disposition. If it is nasty and doesn't allow you to pick it up, don't buy it.

Color

Hamsters today are bred in several different color strains. Most common, after the ordinary golden hamster, are the albino, which is

Two pied hamsters from the same litter differ enough to be told apart.

18

Compare this young guinea pig with a hamster. It weighs 18 ounces, while a hamster of the same age would weigh 3½ or 4 ounces.

white with pink eyes; the pied, harlequin or panda, which are all spotted brown or beige on white with dark eyes; and, recently developed, a cream or beige or fawn variety with brown or ruby eyes. This latter type has several names—which are given by individual breeders but have not yet been established by common use.

Of all of them, the most hardy and most reliable is the ordinary golden (or "Syrian") variety. The albinos are also popular as pets, but some albino strains have faulty vision. Some of the "fancy" colors, too, are high strung and difficult to breed.

Price

Be prepared to pay a fair price for your pet. A hamster that costs less than a dollar is not really a bargain. It is true that some pet dealers, especially in highly competitive areas, try to sell hamsters for less than a dollar, but the quality of such an inexpensive animal could not possibly be good.

Hamsters are basically clean animals; here a hamster cleans itself in a corner of its home (in this case a fish tank).

Above: an albino hanmster. The pure white hamster shown below is not a true albino, because its eyes are not pink.

3. HOW TO RAISE A HAMSTER

Your pet hamster wants to explore, to play, to hide, to hoard food, to keep clean with fresh bedding, and to be handled gently. Once you understand your hamster's habits, training will be easy, and you will have a pet you can really enjoy.

Cages

First of all, hamsters like privacy—privacy from humans and also privacy from *all* other animals and *most* other hamsters. A few young specimens of the same sex do well together but an adult female will

A parakeet cage with flat perches and bedding or a nest box added makes a fine home for a pet hamster.

sometimes kill a male who is introduced into her cage when she is not receptive. If you plan to keep several hamsters together in one cage, provide plenty of room, with separate nest boxes or other hiding places. Keep the sexes separate, and watch the hamsters for signs of fighting. If they do fight, separate them.

These hamsters live in a wooden box with screen stapled on both sides.

Pet hamsters can be kept in special cages manufactured for them and available in pet shops. The cages include water bottles, perches and exercise wheels.

If you prefer, you can make a wooden cage with a screened opening made of wire mesh, ¼ inch square for young hamsters, and no larger than ½ inch for adults. You can also keep your pet in a metal bird cage if you like. If you choose a bird cage, make sure the wires are close together and too strong for the hamster to bend and get out. Generally, the old-fashioned canary cages aren't suitable, but parakeet cages are fine, especially if some of the round perches are replaced with narrow, flat boards.

An empty five-gallon aquarium also makes a suitable hamster home. The top can be wire hardware cloth, galvanized after weaving and weighted to keep your pet in, and other animals like mice, rats, cats, dogs and small boys out.

No matter what type of cage you use, it should have lots of room. Include some kind of device with which the hamster can exercise. A wheel is a useful and attractive addition. Lack of exercise sometimes leads to paralysis.

This acrobatic hamster has managed to climb to the top of the ladder provided for its amusement and exercise.

A handful of baby hamsters; they still have their eyes closed.

The cage should have a secluded area for sleeping and hoarding, and enough space for "toilet facilities" away from the sleeping and hoarding areas. It should have water, draft-free ventilation, and dry, warm cage litter. Wood shavings are best, but torn up newspaper can also be used. Keep the cage away from sunlight or any bright, glaring light. An average temperature of 68°F. is fine.

Unhappy hamsters are usually those that are crowded, not permitted seclusion, deprived of a place to hoard food, or abused by their cagemates. However, even if your hamster has a comfortable home, he may try to escape. This is only the result of his natural curiosity.

Escapes and Captures

The hamster spends a great deal of his time plotting and figuring out ways to escape. He gnaws, digs, scratches, pushes and gnaws some more. And he waits. But at least once he will find his way out, and that's that.

A mother and her babies are very comfortable in this cage. There is lots of space, and privacy in the nest box in the back.

Here is another type of cage for one hamster—an all-glass aquarium. The ½-inch wire mesh provides exercise. Hamsters can climb upside-down with no trouble.

The chances of finding a hamster under the ottoman, in the broom closet, in the piano or television set is about one-half as good as finding the proverbial needle in the haystack. You won't find him by searching, but you can recapture him easily. All you need is a carrot, a deep pail with smooth sides (or a smooth metal wastebasket), and a few bricks or blocks of wood. Another hamster (preferably a female if the escapee is a male) will help. So will some of the wood shavings and nest material taken from the hamster cage. This is what you do. First cover all water closets and aquariums, drain the bathtubs and sinks, and put out the cat. Before you go to bed, set the pail on the floor. Pile the bricks or blocks to form an outside stairway. Rub the carrot up the "steps" and drop it into the pail. Place the wood shavings with the carrot. Put the other caged hamster, if you have one, on the floor alongside the pail. Then go to sleep. In the morning the escaped hamster will be in with the shavings; it happens every time.

Well-furred even at their tender age, these baby hamsters are being carefully tended to by their mother.

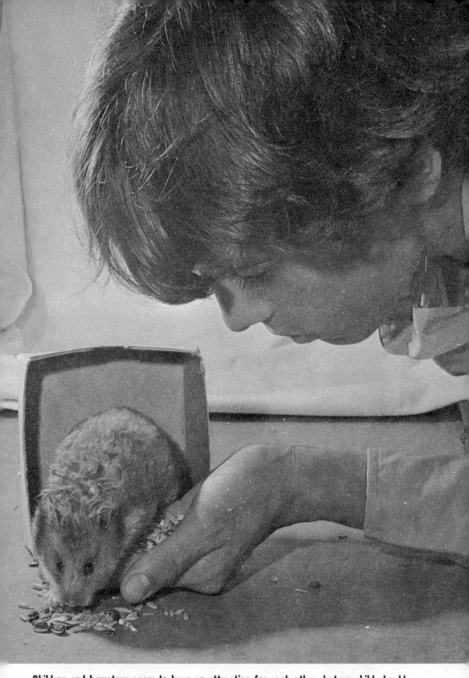

Children and hamsters seem to have an attraction for each other, but no child should have a hamster given into his unsupervised care until he has been given sensible schooling in the humane care and handling of his pet.

If you have any mice in the house and they get trapped with the hamster, he will probably kill them; a rat will almost surely kill the hamster. So don't leave the "trap" any longer than necessary if there are any rats around.

Hamsters are also fond of pipes, tubes, conduits, tunnels and similar long dark spaces.

Even though escape is almost inevitable, you can try to prevent it. Your hamster is not quite quicksilver, but he can get through any opening as large as his head. He's a tiny animal, and rather than risk a loss you should make sure the cage is as strong and tight as possible, with a latch of some sort.

The exercise wheel is more than a luxury, since the activity it affords can prevent paralysis in the hamster. This wheel is about 5 inches wide, with a diameter of about 10 inches.

Hamster Habits

Allow your hamster to crawl out of his cage before you pick him up. As you and your pet become more accustomed to one another, you may find that it is perfectly all right to reach into the cage, but don't do it the first day. When you pick up your hamster, lift his body gently. Don't grasp him by the skin, tail, leg or around the neck. Let him climb into your hand.

Hamsters are nocturnal animals, sleeping during the day. They do not like sunlight or any bright light. However, if you want to play with your hamster during the day he will not object if you awaken him gently, and keep him out of the bright light until he is thoroughly awake. Don't breathe heavily or blow on your hamster. A warning sign is when your hamster's ears are curled or laid back. This often happens when you first waken it or when you disturb a mother hamster. Be patient, and soon the ears will open out and stand erect. Then you can feel reasonably sure that your pet isn't mad at you. Hamsters are naturally friendly with humans, and you will get along well by acting thoughtful and humane.

Easy does it! Hold your hamster gently but firmly, and don't squeeze.

The "baby fur" on this young fawn will soon be replaced by a richer, heavier coat.

Another pied hamster stares curiously at the camera.

The old male hamster's ear is getting shiny and his back is not very straight, but he is still a fine, affectionate pet.

Baby hamsters are not "housebroken." They soil the cage anywhere, but since they are clean animals, by the time they are about two months old their good habits will be well established.

Hamsters have a strong feeling about what is theirs. This applies to their hoards, their homes and their babies. A pet hamster might nip his owner's hand if it is thrust into his nest or even into his cage, but the same animal will be perfectly safe and tame and friendly if he is outside the cage. Sometimes females have a stronger desire to accumulate and hoard food and nesting materials than males. Male hamsters live alone, and do not join in any family affairs. The male may, in fact, destroy the young, or be destroyed himself by the female if he ventures near the babies.

A female hamster that expects young, or a new mother, should be left strictly alone until the babies' eyes are open—when they are about 16 days old. Many litters have been killed or deserted because the pet owner didn't know or didn't have the strength of character to leave the hamsters alone at this time. Of course the first few days are the most crucial, and as time goes on the mother becomes more tolerant.

The hamster's eyesight is not especially good, but his senses of hearing and smell seem to be acute.

Hamsters replace their fur about every three months. As they grow old there is a tendency for less hair to appear on the ears, until at last the ears appear quite shiny.

Golden hamsters hibernate, especially if the air is both moist and cold. If you keep your pet in a cage out of doors, provide a draft-free sleeping area which he can arrange to suit himself during his period of hibernation.

There is a possibility that the life span of the hamster is connected with the amount of hibernation. A hamster that hibernates two months a year may live longer than the 1000 days usually allotted. This is a field that would benefit from study by serious pet keepers.

Food

Hamsters are gnawing animals. They are therefore slow eaters, eaters of seeds, nuts and hard foods. Although they do enjoy soft foods, they are designed and equipped to consume hard materials which are slowly chewed and slowly digested. Because of this hamsters are constant nibblers. This also helps to explain the value of the hoarding instinct and the cheek pouches; hamsters just naturally want to forage for food and carry it, in their pouches, to a hiding place to eat at leisure. If hamsters' food were of a soft, quick-spoiling nature this would not be possible.

Whether you feed your pet once a day at a specified time, or you simply replenish the stock for his hoard when it runs low, it is he who will decide when to eat and what to eat. You may sometimes notice that your hamster is eating when he looks half asleep! It may be that because hamsters, under natural conditions, do most of their eating underground, eyesight is not important for managing their food.

Just because your hamster accepts what you offer and stuffs it into his pouches, it doesn't mean that he plans to eat it soon, or ever. He just wants it, period. It may be something soft for bedding, or perhaps it is something that only a hamster could want.

The best diet for hamsters is a varied one. It should contain fresh raw greens, seeds, nuts, milk, fresh raw fruits, meats, vegetable roots and tubers, insects, eggs and prepared pelleted food. Water is vital but large quantities are not required.

Soft green vegetables and fruits do not lend themselves to pouch-packing and they are often eaten on the spot. They make an excellent

It doesn't seem possible, but this hamster managed to pack away the six additional sunflower seeds before he quit.

diet supplement for hand feeding while you are taming and training your pet.

Most hamster owners feed their pets some sort of pelletized dried vegetable material, available at pet shops. The dried, compressed food is scientifically designed to furnish all the vital substances except water. This is suitable for your hamster's basic diet, but it should be supplemented with some treats—nuts, sunflower seeds, carrots, fruit and meat.

A newborn hamster is nursed by his mother until his fur grows and his eyes open. He should then get soft foods as he is weaned away from his mother's milk. Whole wheat bread soaked in milk is a fine food for baby hamsters and a fine supplemental food for their mothers. Milk sours, and so you should replace this milksop frequently, but you need not be afraid of offering too much of any food to your pets.

That was a nice snack. Now what's for dessert?

Since hamsters will not overeat, you cannot possibly overfeed them. What they do not eat they will hide away. All you must remember is to avoid feeding an excess of food which spoils or smells when it gets old.

Some specific foods you might include in your hamster's diet are: beets, beet tops, bird seed, sunflower seeds, boiled eggs, carrots and carrot tops, live crickets, grasshoppers, corn, corn bread and cracked corn, dog biscuits, milk, lean meat, nuts, oats, potatoes and wheat germ.

All vegetables and fruits should be fresh, raw and washed. (Feed lettuce sparingly because it is a laxative.) Milk should be pasteurized, condensed or evaporated. Citrus fruits are a controversial item of diet; you might try feeding a bit to your hamster and see how he reacts. (Vitamin C is apparently not required in the hamster's diet.) Cooked meats have also been a controversial food for hamsters, with some authorities believing that it induces cannibalism of young by their mothers. Others, however, disagree. Hamsters sometimes like boiled beef bones to grind their teeth on, and they probably derive some vaiue from the minerals in the bone. Dry pellets and dog biscuits, incidentally, are considered a good tooth-grinding medium too.

Wheat germ oil, or substances containing it, is a good addition to the hamster's diet Some pet shops sell ripe whole wheat as it comes from the stalk. This is as good a way as any to assure your pet of Vitamin E. Raw peanuts are also a good source of this vitamin.

Water, of course, is needed by the hamster. Much of it is obtained from the soft foods, but if pellets form a major part of your hamster's diet, a plentiful supply of fresh, clean water is an absolute must. The best way to supply water is from a bottle with a one-hole rubber cork and a bent glass tube, as shown in some of the illustrations. These corks and tubes are available at many pet shops.

If, instead, you leave water in a dish in the cage, your hamster may decide that it is just the place to hoard his food or leave his droppings. In either case the result is messy.

Your hamster needs food, water and certain vitamins to stay healthy and happy.

Hoarding

Your hamster wants to hoard his food. A female with young is especially active in this hoarding business. A nervous hamster, or one who has been recently moved, or one whose cage has just been cleaned, will also stuff his pouches until they look like they will burst.

An adult hamster will keep the hoard in one place in his cage and will try to keep it as far as possible from the spot where he leaves his droppings. Try not to disturb the hoard when you clean the one soiled area in the cage.

Do not change the litter or dispose of the hoarded food more often than once a week, and preferably less often. This is especially important in the case of a female with young. Your sense of smell, at any rate, will be the best guide to how often you have to clean the cage thoroughly. You will find that a hamster cage (or even a hamster colony with thousands of cages) is practically odorless.

After your hamster has fully packed his pouches and carried his prize home he will often use his forepaws to help push from behind to unload the cargo.

4. BREEDING HAMSTERS

If you plan to breed hamsters, you will have an exciting experience. One of the great joys of pet-keeping is having your pets reproduce and watching the young grow to maturity.

Hamsters are noted for their remarkable rate of reproduction. Their period of gestation, 16 days, is the shortest of any known animal. The female is in season and receptive to breeding every 4 days. Litters range from 2 to 15, with 8 the usual number of hamster cubs born. Their development is very rapid, and maturity is reached in less than 3 months. It's even possible to breed a hamster cub 1 month old, although this is not recommended. Weaning is generally at about 5 weeks, and 3 to 7 days after weaning the female can be bred again. Thus you can see that hamster production can be exceedingly great.

These newborn babies are blind and helpless, but the only care they need is from their mother.

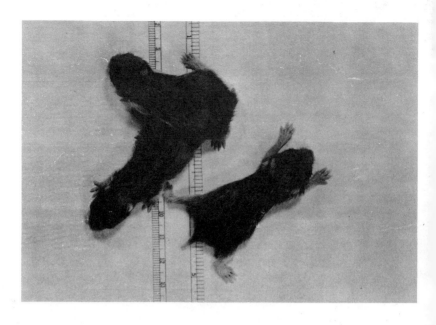

At two weeks old, the babies' eyes are not quite ready to open.

The young are born blind, naked, helpless. They are about one inch long and weigh $1/14$ to $1/8$ of an ounce. After about 10 days the young begin to move about the cage and nibble soft foods, although they still cannot see. Their eyes open when they are about 16 days old.

For breeding purposes you should start with 4- to 6-month-old stock. Provide the female with a cage containing a nest box and soft, clean nesting material. The nest box can be a compartment in a secluded part of the cage. It need not be much larger than a cigar box (no top is needed). Washed rags, tissue paper and pine wood shavings are all good nesting materials.

Test or Trial Breeding

Take the female from her cage and place her in the male's cage during the evening. Females are most receptive to breeding between 9 and 11 P.M. If possible, use an older, larger, experienced male. The female will either attack the male or they will mate before the night is over. If she does attack him, put her back in her own cage and try again the next evening. Repeat nightly until she is receptive. If both hamsters are in good health, this usually happens within a week.

A breeding pair of hamsters in their nest.

These sleeping baby hamsters are huddled together for warmth and security.

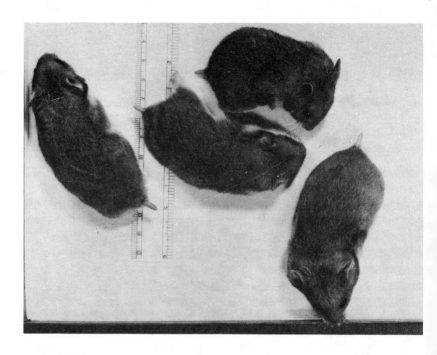

These babies were just weaned. Hamsters should be separated before their 35th day to keep them from breeding.

Pair Breeding

Pair breeding occurs when you simply put a pair together and keep them in the same cage until the female appears pregnant. This technique usually results in a badly abused male. The female will steal his food, scratch and bite him, evict him from his sleeping area, and in extreme cases she may seriously injure or kill him.

In test or pair breeding, if a virgin female receives a male but does not become pregnant, do not give up trying to breed her until a second trial is made. Some virgin hamsters do not become pregnant with the first mating.

Colony Breeding

Some commercial breeders use a technique called colony breeding. A large cage is set up with plenty of nesting material, several water bottles, and possibly a few small nest boxes as hiding places.

Three full-grown mature males are introduced to the cage. After they become thoroughly accustomed to it—after a day or so—about a half-dozen females are placed in the cage with them. Unless there are really serious fights, the animals are confined together until the females swell or until 10 or 11 days have passed. They should all be separated by the 12th day. Don't add any new females until all those in the cage are removed. Then the three males rest a week and another six females are introduced.

The males *must* be permitted to rest at least a week between batches of females, and each female must be placed in a separate cage to bear her young.

Whatever breeding method you use, be sure the female is in her "maternity cage" at least four days before the babies are due. Don't move her until at least three weeks after they are born, and it's better if you wait four or five and the babies are weaned and go their separate ways. Then wait another few weeks before breeding the female again.

Remember that about the time the hamster is weaned, it is sexually mature, and although it should not be bred until it is 4 to 6

Mother seems very content with her 2-week-old litter. The cubs are wandering about, but their eyes are still closed. Note the water bottle spout.

months old, it is capable of breeding. Therefore the sexes should be separated early, before their 35th day at the longest. They will then weigh about 30 grams (approximately 1 ounce). A young female, to properly deliver and nurse all her first litter, should weigh at least 100 grams (3⅓ ounces) before she is bred. A fully mature, healthy breeder must weigh 150 to 158 grams (5-5¼ ounces). If you want to be scientific in your breeding work, you should have an accurate scale or balance graduated in quarter-ounces up to 8 ounces, or in grams to about 200 grams. Some small postage scales do nicely.

Color Varieties

The hamster's normal golden color is subject to some slight variation. Some strains tend to be yellower, others darker. Bellies are sometimes white, gray, yellow-white or blue-white. These differences are slight, and are of little interest to the casual hamster keeper. However, the serious breeder can intensify a color trait and eventually create a color which varies enough to be distinctive.

This full-pouched golden hamster is using its front feet to excavate seeds from among a nest of wood chips.

A mother albino hamster carrying one of her babies.

In addition to these slight differences, there are several different, stand-out color strains. The albino hamster has white fur and pink eyes. The trait is recessive. Only a pair of albinos can produce a 100 per cent albino offspring. However, two golden hamsters can produce an albino by the very rare process of mutation. This is the result of a violent genetic change and each time it occurs a new strain of albinos could be established. This has already happened several times. Albino offspring can also result from the mating of golden parents if, by a rare coincidence, both parents have recessive albino genes.

Another color variation is the "pied," "harlequin," or "panda" hamster. This too is the result of genetic mutation. The markings are variable, with each strain different from other strains, and even individual hamsters vary in coloring from their nestmates. Some are gray-gold mottled on white; others are gold on white, and still other color combinations have been seen.

Pandas tend to be high strung and, if you are a beginning hobbyist, you should not choose them as your first pair to breed, since they require more care than the others.

Each color variety—golden, albino, panda—can be bred to each other. The results will not be hybrids, but merely mixed strains. These mixed strains might bring more vigor to a panda or albino line, but to re-establish the recessive color trait, selective inbreeding must be done.

When breeding hamsters, aim for rich, dense fur; broad, round bodies; bold eyes; erect, uncreased ears; straight backs, and good dispositions. If you are careful about diet, care, and choice of breeding stock, your results should be very satisfactory.

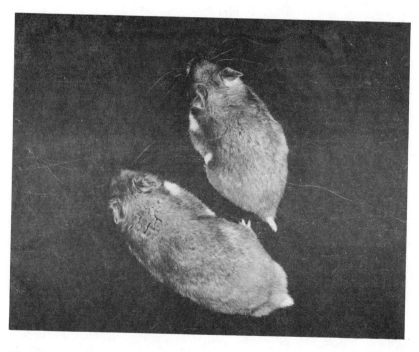

The larger hamster is the male. There is a bulge at the base of his tail, while the female's body tapers smoothly to her tail.

5. COMMERCIAL TRICKS AND TECHNIQUES

Scattered over the country are several hundred professional hamster breeders. The author visited a typical small establishment and while he made the photographs he discussed some of the special problems of hamster production with the proprietor of Rocky Hill Farms in Monsey, New York, Mr. William Lees.

Also present was Mr. Joseph Stocker, of Ramsey, New Jersey. Mr. Stocker is a laboratory animal jobber. As a jobber he performs the important function of assuring a fluctuating market of a steady supply. Schools and some university laboratories shut down in the summer, and other organizations performing research also vary their requirements either seasonally or according to their research programs. Mr. Stocker anticipates these needs and arranges with breeders to have stock of certain size available to meet the demand.

Mr. Lees has several buildings on his property where he raises mice and hamsters. The greatest part of his production, typically, is for research. This calls for normal golden hamsters. The other color varieties are almost completely limited to the demands of the pet trade and the natural human curiosity of men like Mr. Lees.

Mr. Lees keeps his hamster colony in a building which is heated in the winter. It is well insulated not only for winter warmth but also for summer coolness. If the building were cold in winter the hamsters would hibernate and there would be no production. Warm weather also makes hamsters sleepy, and very warm temperature brings on a condition of deep sleep which is much like winter hibernation. The animals are then so limp and quiet that they actually appear at first glance to be dead. The Syrian climate is hot during the day, but during the day the hamster is asleep, deep in his burrow. At night when it is cool the hamster comes out to forage for grain and greens. Thus you see that it is normal for your pet to sleep during the day. If he sleeps "like dead" day and night, you might try to find a more temperate place for his cage.

Mr. Lees suggested that if a pet keeper has a problem with a female who eats her young he should suspect that she is suffering from a diet deficiency, probably calcium and protein. Feed her milk, dog biscuits, and fresh or dried peas and beans.

If she smothers, deserts, or otherwise kills her young but does not eat them, Mr. Lees suggests that she probably did this out of nervousness. This often happens if she feels insecure through lack of adequate bedding, lack of privacy from humans and other hamsters, or lack of milk to feed her babies. First litters from young or undernourished mothers are sometimes killed, but after adequate rest and feeding the same female will produce large healthy litters and raise them to maturity with no trouble.

Mr. Lees keeps his hamsters in wooden, screened cages. Water comes from the standard bottle-and-tube arrangement. Bedding and nest material is pine wood shavings. Food includes animal pellets supplemented with grain and raw, fresh, clean vegetables.

One rule Mr. Lees suggests concerning vegetables is to feed your hamster only what you would serve on your own table. Do not use wilted, dirty, or stale vegetables. Diarrhea is only one of several diseases a hamster may get from second quality greens.

Another hint from Mr. Lees concerns the feeding of soft or

This hamster house has both an exercise wheel and a platform that can be reached by climbing a little ladder.

Curious and appealing, a pet hamster is an animal to which people can form an attachment.

Exercise wheels are inexpensive and easily available, as they are sold in pet shops everywhere. Exercise wheels designed specifically for use with hamsters and other small mammals generally are safer and last longer than homemade wheels.

sticky foods. White bread and rolled oats might be wholesome to eat, but, as you will learn later on, if they are picked up by a hamster and stuffed into the pouches they may get stuck, sometimes back near the shoulder, and cause the eyes to tear. "Prepared" foods like cake, bread, crackers, meal and rolled oats are not part of the natural adult hamster diet and should not be hoarded in the pouches. By contrast a grain of dry corn, wheat or a sunflower seed is smooth and slippery and can be easily pushed out of the pouch when the hamster is ready to hide it or to eat it.

Some of the points Mr. Lees and Mr. Stocker brought up were not primarily concerned with commercial production but are rather tricks and techniques which any pet keeper should know about, and it is a tribute to these men that they are willing to pass on information which bears so directly on their livelihood.

6. HAMSTERS IN RESEARCH

Hamsters have proved valuable in research for several reasons. They are easy to keep, easy to breed, and easy to infect with human diseases. They respond to many diseases in the same way humans do, and they can often be cured with the same drugs. This makes them wonderful research tools. They have been used at one time or another for studies of bomb radiation, tooth decay, reproduction, hormones, influenza, tuberculosis, leprosy, diet, and cancer.

Racks of cages, each with water, pellets, wood shavings and identification tag hold part of the hamster stock at the Sloan-Kettering Institute for Cancer Research. Bottles and cages are sterilized weekly.

A typical hamster pose: two hamsters inspecting each other nose to nose.

The author visited the laboratory of Dr. Joseph G. Fortner at Sloan-Kettering Institute for Cancer Research in New York City and discussed in layman's terms some of the research in cancer currently being performed with the aid of the hamster.

The hamsters used in this particular project are all of the "Syrian" color variety. They are from one strain, bred no closer than third cousins by a commercial breeder. Dr. Fortner uses both sexes and specifies how many of each sex, and the size range he desires for

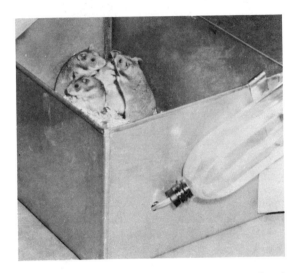

Five hamsters in their laboratory cage at Sloan-Kettering. It is stainless steel and the cover is heavy quarter-inch wire mesh. Note the mounting of the water bottle.

each shipment. The sexes are kept separate and no hamsters are bred for this research project except when the problem is directly related to pregnancy or lactation. Very likely the cost of producing the same number of specimens at the hospital laboratory would cost several times what the commercial breeder can ship them for.

When a shipment arrives the animals are placed in stainless steel cages. Three to five youngsters of one sex or one old specimen to a cage seemed to be the average. These cages are about 12" x 18" by 8" high. The hamsters are fed on pellets, sunflower seeds, carrots, rolled oats and water. The food pellets are thrown in with pine wood shavings and these shavings are changed twice a week. This is simple, clean, and easy. The laboratory is kept at about 72°F. and the animals thrive.

Miss Alice Gale, Dr. Fortner's research assistant, performed several autopsies and several transplants of cancerous tissue while the author took the pictures.

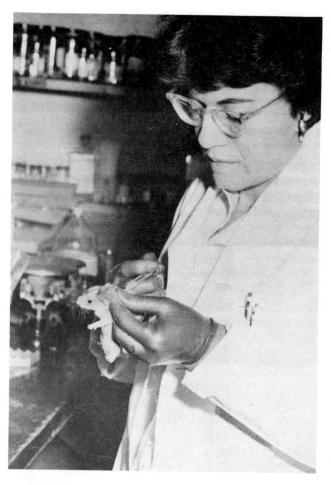

Miss Alice Gale injects a hamster in the course of cancer research. The technique she uses is painless and humane. She believes that love for the animals is necessary to be successful in animal research.

For the autopsies Miss Gale first humanely sacrifices the animal. This is done quickly and painlessly. Then she performs an operation which is technically very similar to an operation on a human being. Equipment is kept sterile and operating room disciplines are maintained.

The transplants of cancerous tissue were accomplished by mincing the tissue obtained from the autopsy and injecting a suspension of it, with terramycin and/or penicillin, into a living specimen. These

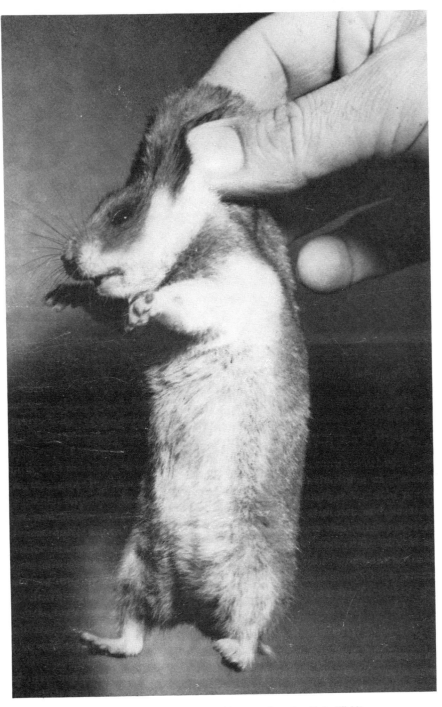

This is the proper method of picking up a hamster that still bites.

Fish tanks can make suitable homes for hamsters and have a special value in that they don't allow drafts to play directly over the animals confined in them.

latter drugs are administered only to reduce the chance that any bacterial infection, separate from the cancer, might also be injected. This transplanting is performed without any great discomfort to the hamster.

Some of the cancers at Dr. Fortner's laboratory have been transplanted as many as *thirty times,* and all this in a space of *less than two years!* A tumor the size of a Concord grape can develop in as short a space of time as two weeks or even ten days. If the same research were performed without the help of these animals, but only through observations on humans, it might take one hundred years instead of one hundred weeks to observe the course of the disease in as many individual specimens. Here is an example of how medical research has been speeded up by this furry little immigrant from Syria.

Hamsters are subject to a number of diseases and ailments. Luckily, remedies and preventives are available at most pet shops.

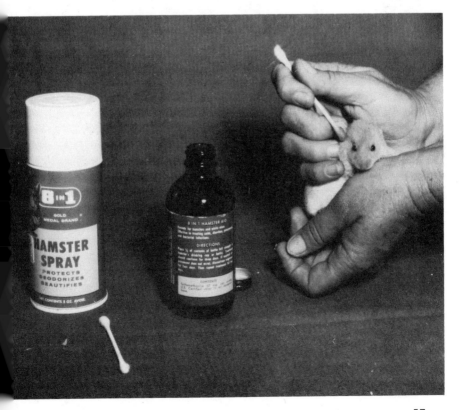

Be careful to observe the interaction between two strange hamsters that you confine together in the same cage. Strange hamsters often fight and the loser might get a severe mauling.

Opposite page, upper photo:
Hamsters are not heavy drinkers, but their water must be fresh and clean at all times. Never let the water in a hamster's bottle grow stale and dirty.

Opposite page, lower photo:
Not every hamster is equally amenable to taming because hamsters vary in temperament. Here a child is attempting to make a hamster tame by gradually introducing it to being handled. All such handling must be gentle.

7. HAMSTER DISEASES

Hamsters live about 1000 days, and with proper care they should never be sick. If your hamster does become sick, treat him with simple, intelligent care.

The symptoms of a *cold* are inactivity and ears held against the head. The hamster's nose may appear swollen because he ruffles his fur when wiping the nasal discharge. In advanced stages he will sniffle and sneeze, get thin, and his fur will lose its luster. Treat cold and sniffles with plenty of fresh, wholesome foods, a clean cage, and warm, dry bedding.

Diarrhea is an intestinal disorder brought on by sudden over-feeding of soft vegetables and fruits, or spoiled foods. The cure comes with a clean cage and a wholesome, balanced diet.

A wet tail is a sign of constipation. *Constipation* in young or adult hamsters is directly related to the amount of pellets and water fed. If you give your hamster pellets, you must provide plenty of fresh water. If you have more than one hamster, make sure that one bossy animal does not take all the water. In case constipation does occur, give youngsters milksop and greens; give adults carrots, leafy vegetables and fruit.

Running eyes sometimes indicate trouble in the cheek pouches, which may be stuffed with such food as bread or rolled oats that gets stuck back near the shoulder. Tears then form in the eye on the side where the stuck particle is. If this happens, flush out the pouch with water of the hamster's body temperature, using a syringe. Try to get your pet to eat soft foods when they are given, instead of stuffing his pouches with them.

Overgrown teeth should be snipped down with a nail clipper, and your hamster should have a bone to gnaw on.

Hamsters enjoy greenfoods occasionally and benefit from eating things like lettuce and celery, but greenfoods should not be fed to the exclusion of other foods; they are more a tonic or treat than a bulk staple item of diet.

This is just one reason why pet hamsters should be accommodated in a safe home. Other household pets might very well be friendly to hamsters or at least tolerant of them—but they might not be!

Overgrown nails may be hereditary. Clip them, but not down to the blood vessel. If you plan to breed hamsters, don't mate any that have overgrown nails.

One form of *paralysis* may result from lack of Vitamin D. Feed wheat germ and wheat germ oil. Other forms of paralysis are the result of lack of exercise. Keep your pet in a roomy cage, with an exercise wheel or some other amusement that will provide activity. Slight paralysis can be cured by such exercise and more fresh foods added to the hamster's diet. There is not much you can do if your pet develops heavy paralysis, so it is wisest to provide the big cage and wheel to prevent it.

Vermin and skin disorders are generally associated with dirty cages. Golden hamsters are desert animals—they don't bathe or swim by choice. But they do keep themselves clean, spending about 20 per cent of their waking hours licking and grooming themselves. They prefer dry quarters and dry fur, and if their cages are clean and dry, with a good supply of nesting litter of shavings, straw, or other dust-free material, they will stay clean and vermin-free.

There is a fly, much like a housefly, which may deposit its eggs on nursing mothers or baby hamsters. The maggots dig into the hamster's flesh and steal milk. If there are such flies in your area, you should use fine screen on the hamster cage and remove any maggots you find. Fortunately, this species of fly is rare.

Infertility is sometimes caused by cold or not enough Vitamin E in the diet. Hamsters that are constantly annoyed, and hamsters that are too fat, may also be infertile. In some recently developed new color strains of hamsters, infertility may be a hereditary weakness.

Stillbirths or death during childbirth are often the result of falls or rough handling of the mother. Injuries which have gone unnoticed often make normal delivery impossible.

If your hamster has a *tumor, internal bleeding* or *skin lesions,* the best thing to do is to have the vet put him to sleep.

The Old Hamster

The hamster leads a short but intense life. Any hamster that lives more than 1000 days or about two years and nine months is a rather exceptional specimen. A three-year-old hamster is a rarity.

If your pet suffers from any incurable disease in his old age, you should bring him to your vet for a painless death. You can be sure that the Nembutal, ether or chloroform used will be painless to the animal, and it is far more humane than letting him suffer.

APPENDIX

The golden hamster was first described in 1839 by Waterhouse and he named it *Cricetus (mesocricetus) auratus.*

meso	= middle-sized (from the Greek)
cricetus	= hamster (from the Latin)
auratus	= golden (from the Latin)

Thus we have the middle-sized golden hamster. In 1941, one hundred and two years later, Ellerman pointed out that *Mesocricetus* is actually a distinct genus and so our hamsters' name, as of 1941, is somewhat more properly *Mesocricetus auratus auratus.*

In the tree of life one way to locate the golden hamster is roughly as follows:

Phylum	— *Chordata*	— with a spinal cord
Class	— *Mammalia*	— nurse young
Subclass	— *Eutheria*	— with placenta
Cohort	— *Glires*	— resembling the dormouse
Order	— *Rodentia*	— chisel-like front teeth
Suborder	— *Myomorpha*	— rats, mice and their allies
Suborder	— *Simplicidentata*	— one pair of upper chisel teeth—this eliminates the rabbits
Superfamily	— *Muroidea*	— mouse-like burrowing animals with some technicalities concerning their teeth which set them apart.
Family	— *Cricetidae*	— hamsters and voles
Subfamily	— *Cricetinae*	— hamsters and their allies
Subfamily	— *Sigmodontinae*	— this is a classification which really refers more to American white-footed mice, etc. (It is mentioned here simply because it appears in some of the older literature.)
Tribe	— *Cricetini*	— hamsters (another technical division)
Genus	—*Mesocricetus*	— middle-sized hamster
Species	— *auratus*	— golden
Subspecies	— *auratus*	— golden